'Written with a strong youth voice element running through.
Unique and very honest.'

Sharon Mee, CEO and Founder of Artpod and Melting Pot – Arts and Wellbeing in Education, Sussex and South East.

I Just Can't Decide!

This colourful, engaging, gender neutral story, introduces the reader to a child overwhelmed with all of life's choices. Should they sit with their friends or befriend someone new? Should they share what they know or keep it to themselves? Should they listen to their heart or follow the crowd?

Written with honesty and a clear youth voice, *I Just Can't Decide!*:

- looks at the challenge of making choices
- champions the courage to make your own choices
- promotes listening to your heart, intuition and body, in addition to your mind
- teaches children about conscious behaviour and self-reflection
- explores ideas of integrity, values and right action
- ends with a mindful reflection, to help children explore and be with their feelings.

This book is essential reading for teachers, parents, or anyone working with children, who wishes to empower young people to make good choices, with sensitivity and self-awareness.

Anita Kate Garai is a teacher, writer and mindful wellbeing consultant.

I Just Can't Decide!

Exploring the Challenge of Making Choices

Anita Kate Garai

Illustrated by Pip Williams

Routledge
Taylor & Francis Group

LONDON AND NEW YORK

Cover illustration credit: © Pip Williams

Logo and 'bubbles' design © 2022 Liz Tui Morris, www.bolster.co.nz

First published 2023

by Routledge

4 Park Square, Milton Park, Abingdon, Oxon OX14 4RN

and by Routledge

605 Third Avenue, New York, NY 10158

Routledge is an imprint of the Taylor & Francis Group, an informa business

© 2023 Anita Kate Garai

Illustrations © 2022 Pip Williams

The right of Anita Kate Garai to be identified as author, and Pip Williams to be identified as illustrator, of this work has been asserted in accordance with sections 77 and 78 of the Copyright, Designs and Patents Act 1988.

British Library Cataloguing-in-Publication Data

A catalogue record for this book is available from the British Library

Library of Congress Cataloging-in-Publication Data
Names: Garai, Anita Kate, author. | Williams, Pip (Illustrator), illustrator.
Title: I just can't decide! : exploring the challenge of making choices / Anita Kate Garai ; illustrated by Pip Williams.
Description: 1 Edition. | New York, NY : Routledge, 2022.
Identifiers: LCCN 2021051870 (print) | LCCN 2021051871 (ebook) | ISBN 9781032233963 (paperback) | ISBN 9781003280149 (ebook)
Subjects: LCSH: Choice (Psychology) in children—Juvenile literature. | Decision making—Juvenile literature. | Self-consciousness (Awareness)—Juvenile literature.
Classification: LCC BF723.C47 G37 2022 (print) | LCC BF723.C47 (ebook) | DDC 153.8/3—dc23/eng/20211222
LC record available at https://lccn.loc.gov/2021051870
LC ebook record available at https://lccn.loc.gov/2021051871

ISBN: 978-1-032-23396-3 (pbk)

ISBN: 978-1-003-28014-9 (ebk)

DOI: 10.4324/9781003280149

Typeset in Londrina
by Apex CoVantage, LLC   Printed in the UK by Severn, Gloucester on responsibly sourced paper

To Emma and Tilds

I just can't decide! I don't know what to do.

I have choices to make, but I haven't a clue.

or should I go right?

Should I go left,

2

Should I let go,

or should I just figh

Should I say yes,

or should I say no?

I'm always so worried

what people will say.

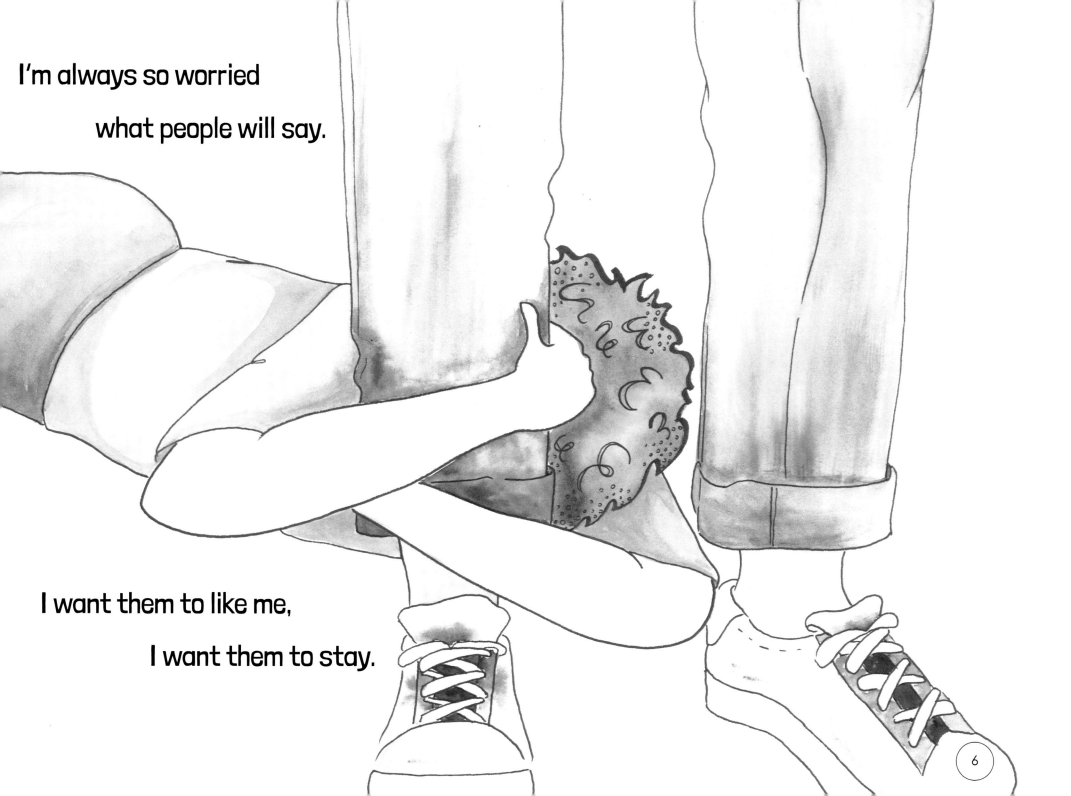

I want them to like me,

I want them to stay.

At school when I go into lunch, I can see
my friends are all crazily waving at me

But Christopher's sitting there all on his own. Should I sit with him,

so he's not alone?

And what should I do when my nan comes to stay

and gives me a look that says 'Please go away.'

I see tears in her eyes and it makes me feel s

9

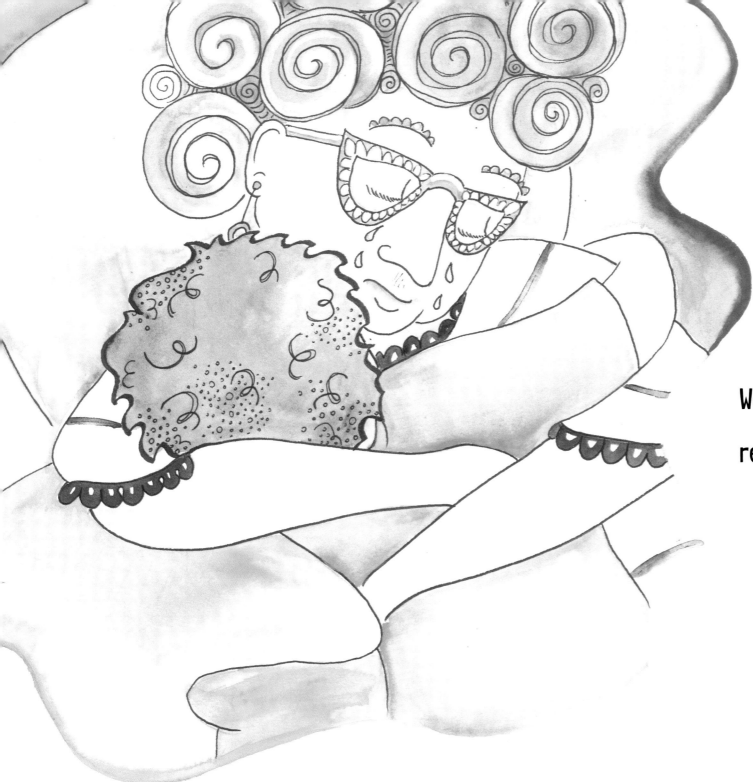

Would **_not_** going away,

really be all that bad?

My brother is fuming 'cos

he has just seen

that
someone
has
broken
his
favourite
screen.

I'm feeling so heavy with shoulds and should nots,

my mind keeps on whirring, my face has grown spots.

When I think and I think it confuses me so . . .

the more that I think,

the less that I know.

14

When it comes to a problem like 60 x 20

my mind jumps into action – it knows

what to do (sometimes!)

But when somebody's feelings depend

on my choice,

that's when it's time to give my heart

a voice.

While my mind can remember the

words of a song,

my heart can tell me when

something *feels* wrong.

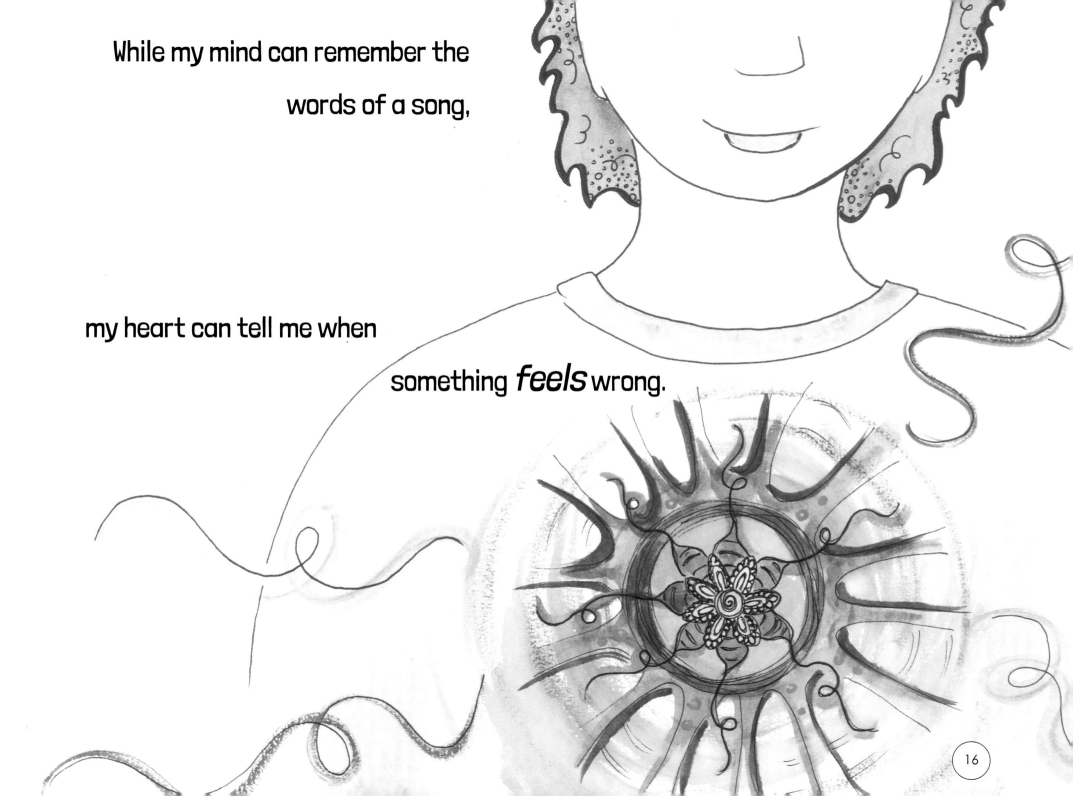

So instead of just asking my mind

to decide,

I put my hand on my heart, and ask

deep down inside.

My heart gives me answers my mind may

not know.

It helps me get clearer on

which

way

to

go.

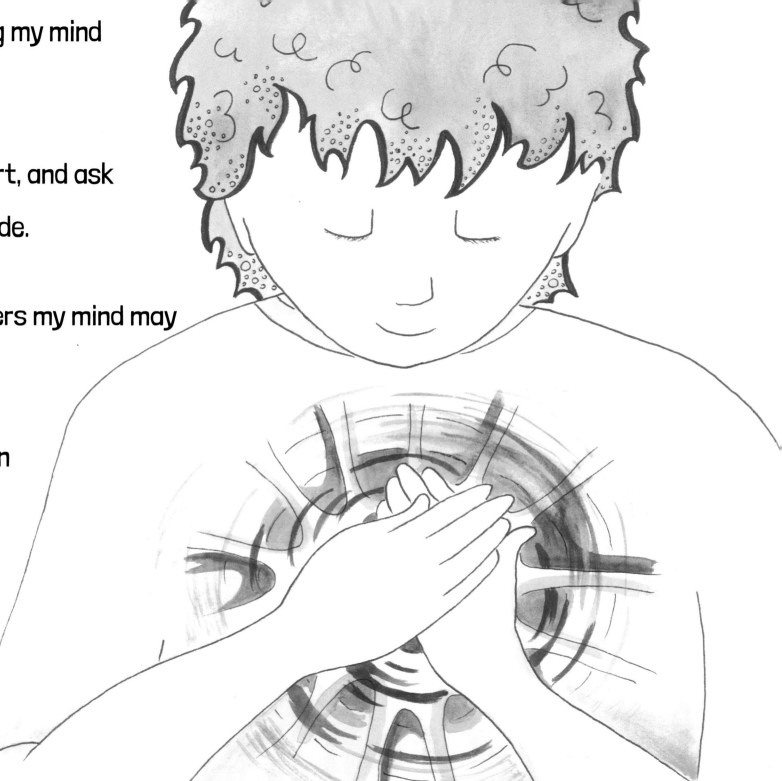

next time YOU need to decide what to do, I recommend giving your heart a chance too.

And if your head feels too full
and your heart feels like jelly . . .

you could always try

asking your

feet

or your belly!

Reflection

It can take a lot of courage to make our own choices. Think of a choice that you found (or are finding) difficult to make.

As you reflect on this, notice how it feels in your body:

> Does the feeling have a colour?

> Does it have a shape?

> Does it have a movement?

> Does it have a sound?

More reflections, activities and explorations are available in *Being With Our Feelings – A Mindful Approach to Wellbeing for Children: A Teaching Toolkit* by Anita Kate Garai (Routledge, 2022).